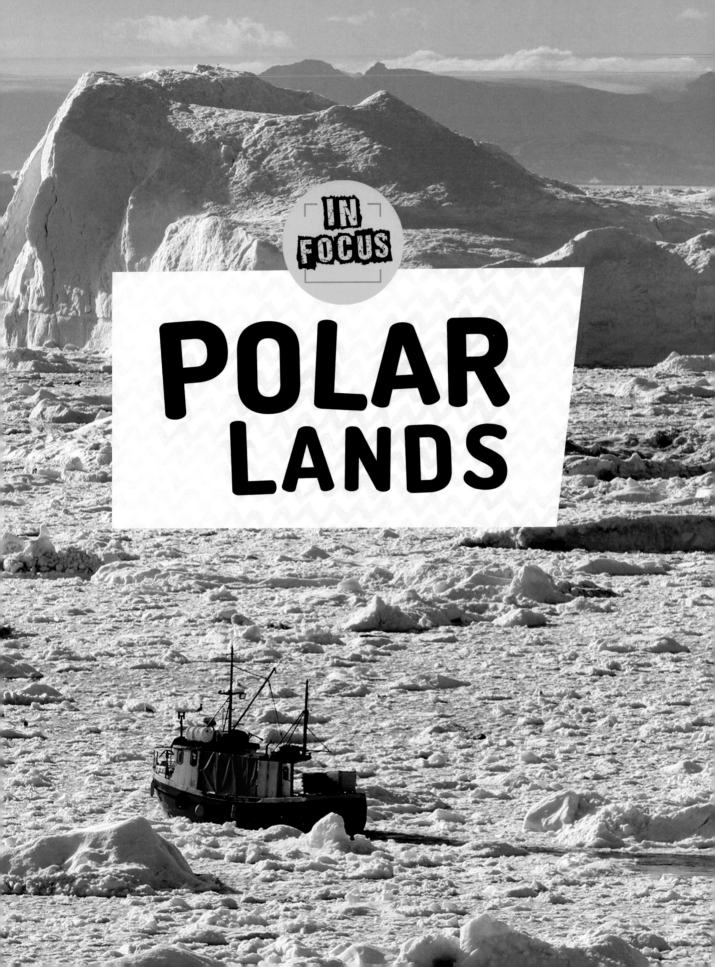

IN FOCUS

POLAR LANDS

KINGFISHER
LONDON & NEW YORK

Distributed in the U.S. and Canada by Macmillan,
175 Fifth Ave., New York, NY 10010.

Library of Congress Cataloging-in-Publication data has been applied for.

Series editor: Hayley Down
Designer: Jeni Child

ISBN (PB): 978-0-7534-7352-8
ISBN (HB): 978-0-7534-7351-1

Kingfisher books are available for special promotions
and premiums. For details contact: Special Markets
Department, Macmillan, 175 Fifth Ave.,
New York, NY 10010.

For more information, please visit
www.kingfisherbooks.com

Printed in China

9 8 7 6 5 4 3 2 1

1TR/0417/WKT/UG/128MA

Picture credits
The Publisher would like to thank the following for permission to reproduce their material.
Top = t; Bottom = b; Middle = m; Left = l; Right = r
Front cover: Getty/Wayne Lynch; Back cover: Shutterstock/Mikael Broms; Cover flap: iStock/KeithSzafranski; Page 1 iStock/carlaexmota; 3 iStock/Grafissimo; 4–5 iStock/Terraxplorer; 4t Shutterstock/Sara Winter; 4b iStock/KenCanning; 5 iStock/kovalchuk; 6 iStock/Terraxplorer; 7t Alamy/blickwinkel; 7m Getty/Hiroya Minakuchi; 7b Alamy/ton koene; 8–9 Shutterstock/Mikael Broms; 10tl Getty/UniversalImagesGroup; 10m Shutterstock; 10b Shutterstock/Avatar_023; 11tm Shutterstock/Pavel Svoboday; 11tr Getty/UniversalImageGroup; 11b Shutterstock/2j architecture; 12 Getty/Bettman; 13t Alamy/Archive Pics; 13m Getty/Bettman; 13b Getty/Bob Haswell; 14b Creative Commons; 15t Alamy/blickwinkel; 15b Alamy/REUTERS; 16–17 iStock/sodar99; 18t Getty/Alasdair Turner; 18bl NASA; 18br Getty/Paul Nicken; 19tGetty/Dymtryo Pylypenko; 19bl Getty Paul Nicken; 19brGetty/Carsten Peter; 20–21 Shutterstock/Dymtryo Pylypenko; 21t iStock/encrier; 22–23 Alamy/Steve Bloom Images; 24 (1) 25tl (2) Alamy/Charlie Summers; 25tl (3) Alamy/Paul Souders; 25ml (4)Shutterstock/Mogens Trolle; 25bl (5) Shutterstock/JoCrebbin; 25bl (6) Shutterstock/Anders Peter Photography; 25tr (7) iStock/KeithSzafranski; 25tr (8) Shutterstock/Natural Earth Imagery; 25mr (9) Shutterstock/Anton_Ivanov; 25br (10) Alamy/Andrew Walmsley; 26–27t Shutterstock/Volodymyr Kyrylyuk; 26tl Alamy/age fotostock; 26tr Alamy/Ilukee; 26bl Shutterstock/Nicram Sabod; 26br iStock/4loops; 27bl Alamy/Steven J. Kazlowski; 27br iStock/Dmitry_Chulov; 28–29 Alamy/blickwinkel; 30 (1) Shutterstock/joCrebbin; 31tl (2) iStock/Lazareva; 31tl (3) Shutterstock/Geoffrey Kuchera; 31ml (4) iStock/LeFion; 31bl (5)Getty/Paul Nicklen; 31bl (6) iStock/KenCanning; 31tr (7) iStock/FRANKHILDEBRAND; 31tr (8) iStock/pilipenkoD; 31mr (9) iStock/Robjem; 31br (10) iStock/richLindie; 32t iStock/SeventhDayPhotography; 32b iStock/mzphoto11; 33t iStock/mzphoto11; 33m iStock/mikeuk; 33b iStock/zanskar; 34–35 Alamy/blickwinkel; 36–37 Alamy/Paul Souders; 37r Alamy/Paulette Sinclair; 38 (1) Shutterstock/Boris Pamikov; 39tl (2) Getty/Paul Nicklen; 39tl (3) iStock/oceanbounddb; 39ml (4) Alamy/blickwinkel; 39bl (5) Alamy/WILDLIFE GmbH; 39bl (6) Alamy/cbimages; 39tr (7) Creative Commons; 39tr (8) Alamy/Norbert Wu; 39mr (9) Alamy/Accent Alaska; 39br (10) Nature PL; 40 Getty/wildestanimal; 41t Alamy/WaterFrame; 41b iStock/PaulWolf; 42–43 Alamy/blickwinkel; 44 iStock/kovalchuk; 45t iStock/icarmen13; 45m iStock/IPGGutenbergUKLtd; 45b iStock/MichaelVacchiano; 46–47 Shutterstock/Kirk Geisler; 48 (1) Getty/Time Life Pictures; 49tl (2) Shutterstock/IgorGolovniov; 49tl (3) Getty/CANOVAS Alvaro; 49ml (4) Alamy/ZUMA Press; 49bl (5) Getty/ Scott Polar Research Institue, University of Cambridge; 49bl (6) Getty/Bettman; 49tr (7) Getty/Gordon Wiltsie; 49tr (8) Creative Commons; 49mr (9) Creative Commons; 49br (10) Getty/LEON NEAL; 50t Creative Commons; 50b Shutterstock/Evgeny Kovalev spb; 51t Creative Commons; 51b Creative Commons; 52–53 (1) Tom McShane Photography; 52br (2)Creative Commons; 52br (3) Creative Commons; 53bl (4) Red Bull; 53bl (5) Creative Commons; 53tr (6)Alamy/William Sutton; 53tr (7) iStock; 53mr (8) AGCO Corp; 53br (9) Getty/Mike Flokis; 53br (10) iStock/Laszlo Szirtesi; 54–55 iStock/SeppFriedhuber; 56t Alamy/robertharding; 56m Getty/Universal History Archive; 57t Shutterstock/Anton_Ivanov; 57m Alamy/John Frost Newspapers; 58 Getty/Galen Rowell; 59t Alamy/Stocktrek Images, Inc.; 59b Alamy/Radharc Images; 60 Shutterstock/Denis Burdin; 61 iStock/KeithSzafranski; 62–63 iStock.

IN FOCUS

POLAR LANDS

BY CLIVE GIFFORD

KINGFISHER
NEW YORK

CONTENTS

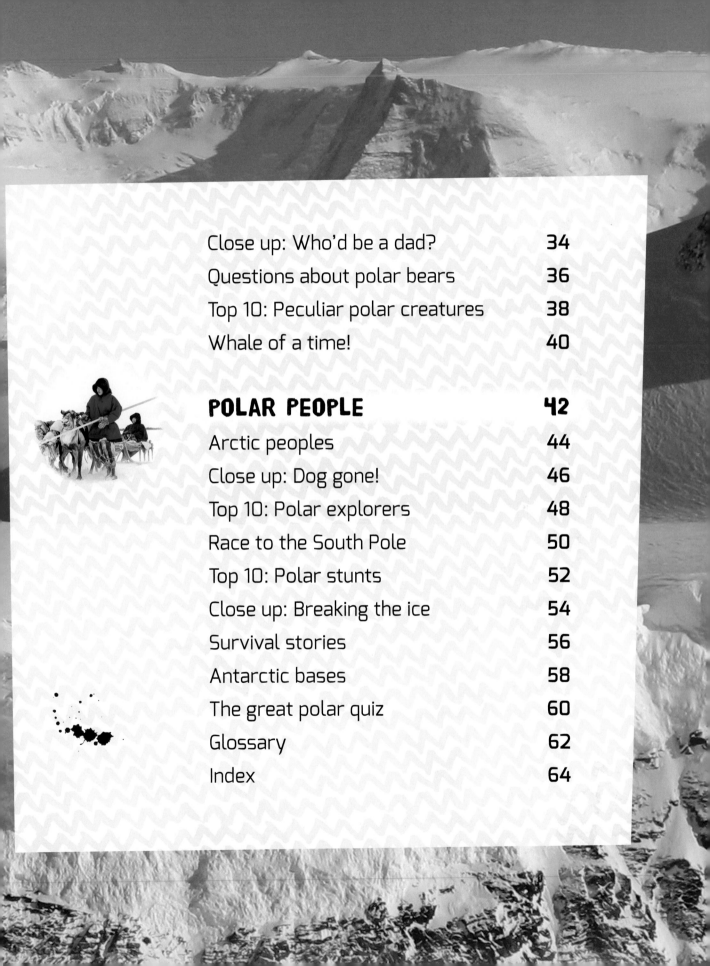

WELCOME TO THE ENDS OF THE EARTH!

The extreme north and south of the planet are known as the North Pole and the South Pole. The land and waters around each pole make up the **polar** regions. In the south is icy Antarctica; in the north, a mixture of Arctic Ocean, ice sheets, and parts of North America, Europe, and Asia.

The polar regions have much in common. The Sun never sets during their summers, and their winters bring bitterly cold temperatures. Yet, despite the hostile conditions, both are home to some incredible creatures and stunning sights!

snow-capped mountains in northern Norway

INSIDE YOU'LL FIND . . .

. . . blue icebergs

EXPERIENCE the geography and climate at the poles and their extraordinary scenery and features, from dazzling light shows to **icebergs** bigger than whole countries!

FROZEN FACT

. . . awesome animals

FROZEN FACT

CHECK OUT seals, penguins, polar bears, and many more fascinating creatures that make the freezing polar regions their home.

. . . polar people

FROZEN FACT

LEARN ABOUT the brave and resourceful people who live in, work in, and explore the polar regions.

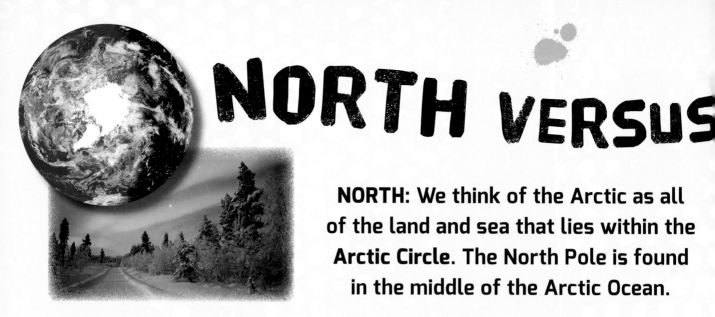

NORTH VERSUS

NORTH: We think of the Arctic as all of the land and sea that lies within the **Arctic Circle**. The North Pole is found in the middle of the Arctic Ocean.

NORTH FACT FILE

Highest point: Mount Gunnbjörn, Greenland (12,119ft., or 3,694 m)
Nearest ocean: Arctic Ocean
Midsummer: June 21
Midwinter: December 21
Highest temp. at North Pole: 41°F (5°C)
Lowest temp. at North Pole: –45°F (–43°C)
Permanent population: 4 million
Biggest settlement: Murmansk, Russia (approx. 307,000 people)

reindeer

ARCTIC PEOPLE

People have lived within the Arctic Circle for thousands of years. Many live **nomadic** lives, moving from place to place hunting and sometimes herding animals. Oil, fishing, mining, and trading have seen some towns founded in the Arctic, including Murmansk, Russia and Tromsø, Norway.

FROZEN FACT

TEMPERATURES lower than –40°F (–40°C) are common in the winter in the Russian Arctic town of Oymyakon. Schoolkids there have to be tough. The school closes only if the temperature plummets to –62°F (–52°C) and it gained its first indoor toilet in 2008!

SOUTH

SOUTH: The Antarctic includes islands, parts of the Southern Ocean, and the continent of Antarctica. The South Pole is in the middle of Antarctica.

SOUTH FACT FILE

Highest point: Mount Vinson (16,050 ft., or 4,892 m)
Nearest ocean: Southern Ocean
Midsummer: December 21
Midwinter: June 21
Highest temp. at South Pole: 56°F (−13.5°C)
Lowest temp. at South Pole: −81°F (−62.8°C)
Permanent population: 0
Biggest settlement: McMurdo Station (approx. 1,200 people)

ANTARCTIC PEOPLES

No one lives permanently in Antarctica but around 4,000–5,000 visitors live and work at bases and science stations on the **continent** during the summer. This number drops to around 1,000 in the winter. In the summer, about 40,000 tourists visit, mostly by ships for short trips.

FROZEN FACT

The **COLDEST** temperature ever recorded on Earth was at the Vostok research station in Antarctica in 1983. It was a bone-chilling, teeth-chattering −128.6°F (−89.2°C)—four times colder than a household freezer!

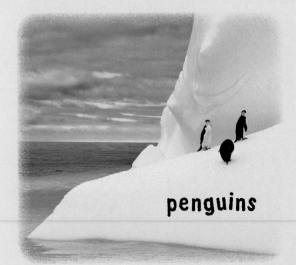

penguins

REACHING THE NORTH POLE

The North Pole can be a confusing place. When people say they have reached it on land, they really mean they are floating above it, on large pieces of ice. And when they have tried to mark the pole's place by placing a flag or sign, they find that, as the shifting sea ice moves, their marker eventually drifts away!

More than one pole

Did you know there's more than one North Pole? There is the magnetic North Pole, which is the place the needle on a compass points to when it indicates north. This is around 300 mi. (500 km) away from the geographic North Pole, the most northerly point of the planet. Will Steger reached the North Pole by dog sled in 1986.

Will Steger

Robert Peary

history mystery

No one is certain who reached the **NORTH POLE** first. Maybe ancient Arctic people, such as the Inuit, or one of the explorers who claimed to reach it in the early 20th century, such as Frederick Cook or Robert Peary.

fly over

The first successful flight over the North Pole was by the airship **NORGE** in 1926. It contained the famous explorer Roald Amundsen. In 1949, two men parachuted down to the pole for the first time—awesome!

underwater exploring

In 1958, the **USS NAUTILUS** made history. This American submarine traveled under the ice to become the first to reach the waters of the North Pole.

ANTARCTIC LANDMARKS

Discover fascinating facts about the geography of Earth's most extreme continent.

* **ANTARCTICA** is the highest continent, with an average height above sea level of 8,200 ft. (2,500 m). The land contains many mountain ranges, including the Transantarctic Mountains, which run across the whole continent.

* The continent contains just one active volcano: **MOUNT EREBUS**.

* Hidden under Antarctica's ice are more than 400 lakes. The largest is called **LAKE VOSTOK** and, with an area of more than 4,800 sq. mi. (12,500 km²), it's bigger than the Mediterranean island of Cyprus!

* The ceremonial **SOUTH POLE**, near the Amundsen-Scott South Pole Station, is marked by a small, red-and-white-striped pole topped with a chrome globe. It is surrounded by 12 flags, representing the countries that agreed to keep Antarctica clean and free of military forces.

* The **ANTARCTIC PENINSULA** is 800 mi. (1,300 km) long—that's almost the distance between New York City and Jacksonville, Florida!

* Taylor Glacier is home to **BLOOD FALLS**, a waterfall full of chemicals that turn its waters a rusty red color.

Where the ice meets the ocean, **ice shelves** form. The largest is the **ROSS ICE SHELF**, which covers an area bigger than California!

There are seven **CHURCHES** on the continent, built by visitors to Antarctica. These include the 147 ft. (45 m)–tall Trinity Chapel on King George Island.

CLOSE UP

NORTHERN LIGHTS

The incredible light display in this picture occurs above a mountain fjord in Greenland. The Northern Lights appear in a large region surrounding the magnetic North Pole and are caused by tiny particles streaming out from the Sun. When these particles collide with Earth's **atmosphere**, a bright light show fills the sky!

What's in a name?

The scientific term for the light display at the North Pole is *Aurora borealis*. It was named by famous astronomer Galileo Galilei in 1619. *Aurora* is the name of the ancient Roman goddess of dawn and *Boreas* is the name of the ancient Greek god of the north wind.

See what scientists get up to on the planet's chilliest continent!

SCIENCE GOES SOUTH

WEATHER MEASURE

Scientists measure the weather all over Antarctica. Below, they are releasing a weather balloon called a radiosonde, which measures the winds and temperatures in the atmosphere. Some Antarctic winds reach more than 155 mph (250 km/h)—faster than most cars!

radiosonde

GOING BACK IN TIME

Ice below the surface of Antarctica was formed many thousands of years ago. Scientists drill cylinders, called ice cores, out of the ice. They analyze what the cores contain to find out what the climate was like in the past. Some of the ice on Antarctica is ancient. In 2006, Japanese scientists recovered an ice core that contained ice thought to be a million years old!

ice core

Scientists use skis and a sled to carry equipment.

ROCK AND ICE

Scientists discover and study fascinating features found in Antarctica's ice and rock. These include startling ice caves (below) and more than 20,000 meteorites (rocks from space). In 2016, a team on James Ross Island, close to the Antarctic Peninsula, found hundreds of fossils of dinosaurs, which lived around 70 million years ago.

ice cave

LIFE ON THE CONTINENT

Some scientists study the wildlife around the coast of the continent. They map populations of seals, penguins, and other creatures, measure the wingspans of birds, and study the birds' habits. They also dive into the freezing waters to explore the ocean floor, even discovering new species (types of animal) on the way!

chilly!

INCREDIBLE
ICEBERGS

**Your questions about
these magnificent chunks
of floating ice answered!**

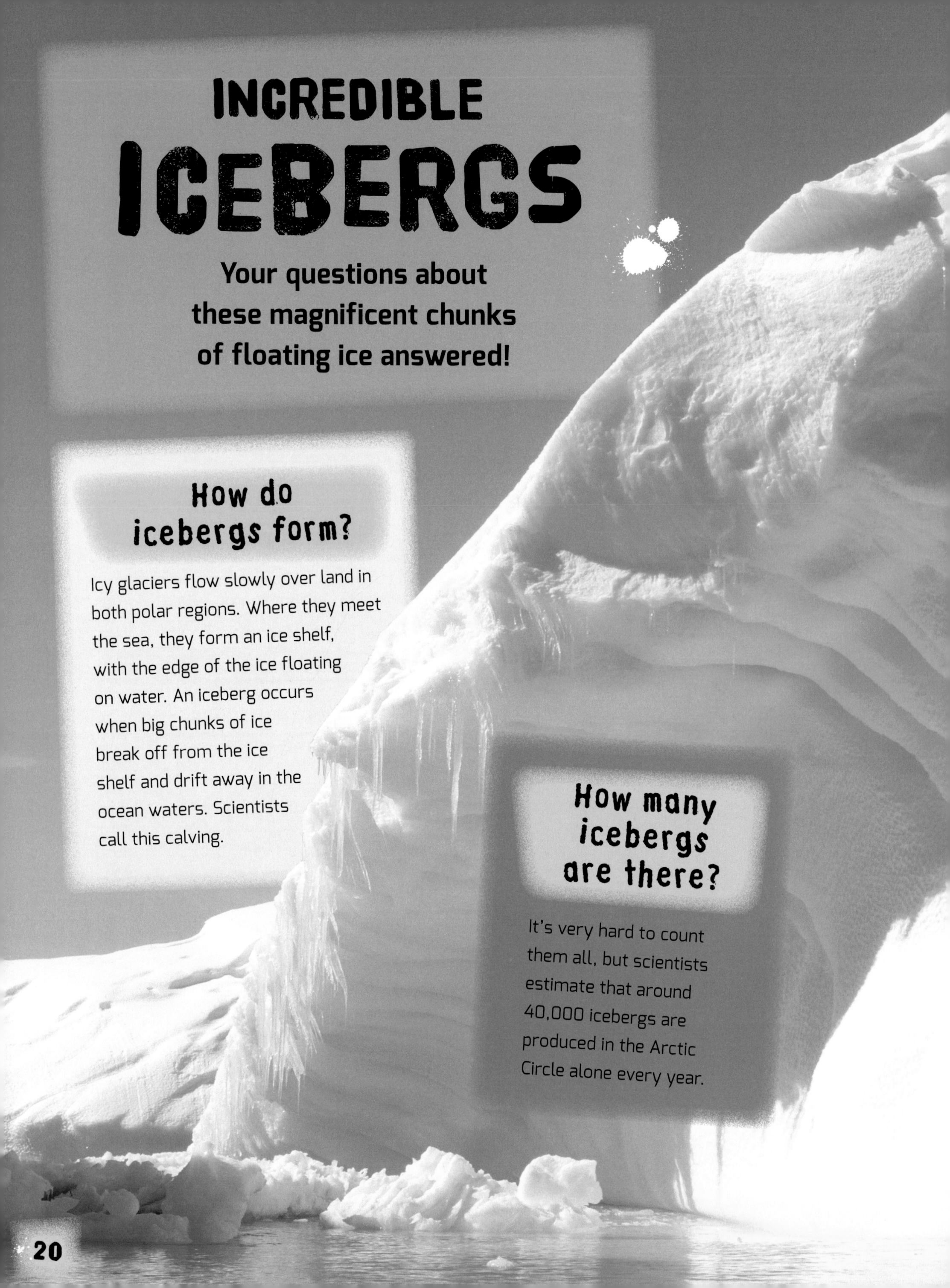

How do icebergs form?

Icy glaciers flow slowly over land in both polar regions. Where they meet the sea, they form an ice shelf, with the edge of the ice floating on water. An iceberg occurs when big chunks of ice break off from the ice shelf and drift away in the ocean waters. Scientists call this calving.

How many icebergs are there?

It's very hard to count them all, but scientists estimate that around 40,000 icebergs are produced in the Arctic Circle alone every year.

How long do icebergs last?

Some icebergs melt away quickly in weeks or months. Others, though, hang around for years! Most circulate in the polar oceans, but a small number travel north from Antarctica or south from the Arctic. In 1926, a small Arctic iceberg was spotted just 130 mi. (210 km) off the coast of the island of Bermuda.

How big are icebergs?

They vary in size from "growlers," which are the size of a car, up to real whoppers! One iceberg spotted in the North Atlantic was 551 ft. (168 m) high—as tall as a 55-story building. The biggest iceberg ever was B-15, which broke off the Ross Ice Shelf in Antarctica in 2000. It had an area of around 4,250 sq. mi. (11,000 km²), bigger than Jamaica!

iceberg in the Arctic Circle

POLAR
CREATURES

PENGUIN SPECIES

There are 17 different species of penguins. Check out 10 of the most fascinating!

1 Emperor

This is the tallest and heaviest penguin, standing up to 3.5 ft. (1.1 m) tall and weighing as much as a typical 12-year-old child! Emperors are the deepest divers, plunging 1,850 ft. (565 m) below the water's surface.

2 King

The second-largest penguin, king penguins are fussy parents, taking 14–16 months to raise a chick!

7 Adélie

This penguin has a white ring around each eye. It is an excellent swimmer, cruising up to 93 mi. (150 km) from its nest.

3 Chinstrap

These penguins love to "toboggan"—skating along the ice on their feathery belly and using their flippers and feet.

8 Magellanic

These penguins are usually found around South America, but some stray onto the Antarctic coast to hunt for seafood.

4 Gentoo

The fastest penguin can race through water four times faster than a human Olympic swimming champion!

9 Macaroni

Thought to be the most common penguin, with some 18 million in the wild. They are easily spotted because of their orange head feathers.

5 Rockhopper

Looking more punk rock than rockhopper, with their wild spiky head feathers, these small but aggressive birds make their nests on the rocky coasts of islands.

10 Little

This is the smallest penguin species, standing just 13 in. (33 cm) tall. It's about the size of a dinner plate.

6 Yellow-eyed

The world's rarest penguin, with just 4,000 thought to exist, is found in and around New Zealand. It can live to be 20 years old!

Which penguin is your number one?

ADAPT TO THE ARCTIC

Many creatures have found ways to survive in the Arctic. Some have special physical adaptations to help them live there.

WARM COAT

Many Arctic animals are protected from the cold by a thick layer of hair or fur. The musk ox's heavy fur coat is made up of two layers: long, thick guard hairs on the outside and a dense layer of shorter hairs underneath. These layers trap air to warm the musk ox's body. Their fur fibers can be spun into *qiviut* wool, which is up to eight times warmer than sheep's wool.

musk ox

COZY HOME

Little lemmings dig deep, narrow burrows in the snow, often 3–6.5 ft. (1–2 m) below the surface. Snow is a good insulator and keeps their burrow temperature warm enough for babies that are born there. The ground squirrel also builds burrows but doesn't stay active in the winter. Instead, it goes into **hibernation**—a sort of deep sleep—for months at a time.

lemming

snow geese

CAMOUFLAGE

The Arctic fox has dark-brown fur in the summer. In the fall, it grows a layer of white fur that makes it hard to spot by potential **prey** as it prowls and hunts in the wintry snow and ice. Arctic hares are also **camouflaged** in white fur so they can hide from **predators**—such as the fox!

Arctic fox

WINTER BREAK

For some creatures, winter in the Arctic is just too much! They head off on journeys, called **migrations**, to find climates they can tolerate. Caribou herds graze in Alaska's **tundra** in the summer, then follow centuries-old trails south to Yukon, Canada, in the winter. Snow geese also head south, flying 1,865 mi. (3,000 km) in flocks.

caribou

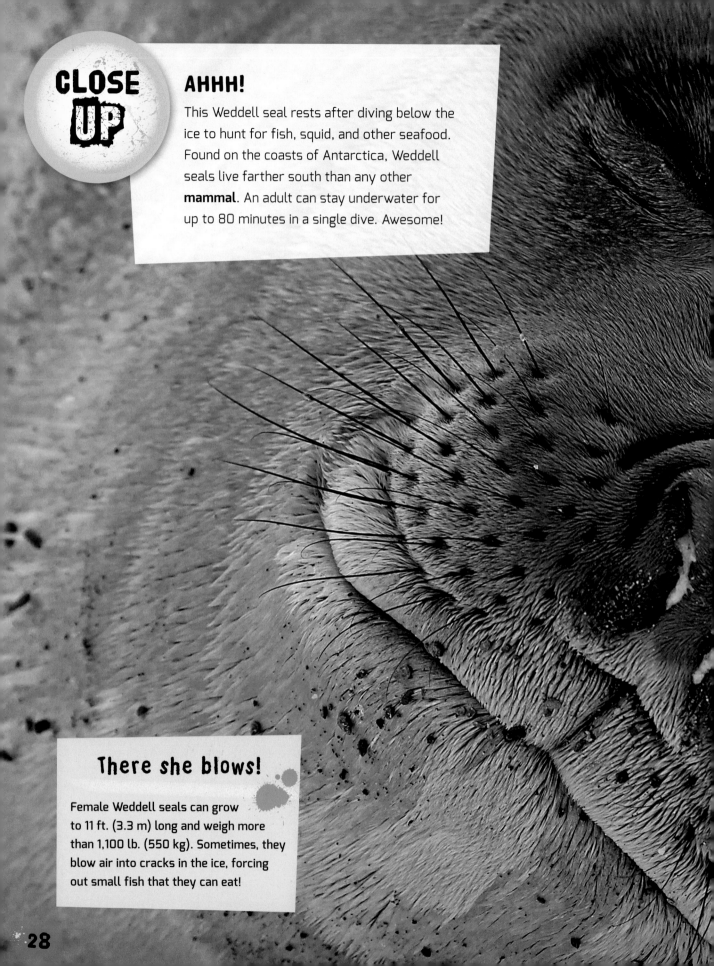

AHHH!

This Weddell seal rests after diving below the ice to hunt for fish, squid, and other seafood. Found on the coasts of Antarctica, Weddell seals live farther south than any other **mammal**. An adult can stay underwater for up to 80 minutes in a single dive. Awesome!

There she blows!

Female Weddell seals can grow to 11 ft. (3.3 m) long and weigh more than 1,100 lb. (550 kg). Sometimes, they blow air into cracks in the ice, forcing out small fish that they can eat!

POLAR HUNTERS

Want to meet the fiercest predators around the poles? You've come to the right place!

Polar bear

Cunning and powerful, the **carnivorous** polar bear stalks the Arctic as the region's top predator. It has excellent eyesight and can sniff out the scent of a seal 1,000 mi. (1.6 km) away. When it strikes, its powerful arms and sharp claws and teeth make quick work of most prey.

2 Killer whale (orca)

Found in both Arctic and Antarctic waters, this toothed hunter sure has a mean streak. It preys on sharks, seals, and even huge whales!

3 Wolverine

These aggressive Arctic animals are just 25.5–39 in. (65–100 cm) long, but they eat far bigger critters, such as moose!

4 Arctic wolf

Wolves attack musk ox, caribou, and Arctic hares with their strong jaws that contain 42 sharp teeth!

5 Greenland shark

Big—at up to 21 ft. (6.4 m) and 1,985 lb. (900 kg)—and beastly, these slow-moving sharks are cold-blooded hunters. They sometimes snap up seals and often feast on fish.

6 Walrus

Powerful lip muscles allow a hungry walrus to crack clam shells and suck up what's inside in seconds. An adult walrus might eat as many as 4,000 a day!

7 Peregrine falcon

A summer visitor to the Arctic, this is the fastest animal on Earth, flying at more than 186 mph (300 km/h) to catch its prey.

8 Leopard seal

These one-ton terrors lie in wait under an icy ledge. Using powerful jaws, they grab passing penguins—up to six a day!

9 Puffins

This Arctic bird can dive to 200 ft. (60 m) underwater. Puffins can store a dozen or more small fish, such as hake, sideways in their big bill.

10 Southern elephant seal

The biggest of all seals, these deep divers plunge more than 0.6 mi. (1 km) below sea level to snack on seafood.

Which polar hunter is your number one?

BEAUTIFUL BIRDS

head turner!

Hundreds of different species of birds can be found in the polar regions. They range from tiny Arctic redpolls, which weigh just 0.5 oz. (15 g), to powerful imperial shags, which can dive down 165 ft. (50 m) into Antarctic waters to feed.

The **SNOWY OWL** can turn its head three-fourths of the way around. Razor-sharp talons, plus strong eyesight and hearing, make it a lethal foe—especially for lemmings, its favorite food!

FROZEN FACT

stinkers!

SOUTHERN GIANT PETRELS reek! They can spit out a foul-smelling oil from their stomach to ward off other creatures. These birds will eat almost anything—including parts of dead seals or whales!

FROZEN FACT

one BIG bird

The **WANDERING ALBATROSS** is the largest flying bird in the world, with a wingspan of up to 11.5 ft. (3.5 m). It glides on the wind above the Southern Ocean, cruising 590 mi. (950 km) in a day!

ARCTIC TERNS leave the Arctic in August and head to Antarctica. They fly back the next June— making migration journeys each year of 24,850–43,500 mi. (40,000–70,000 km).

long-distance champion!

sky pirates

The **SKUA** frequently attacks other birds in midair and plunders their food. This scavenger bird thinks nothing of stealing and eating the eggs or young chicks of other birds.

WHO'D BE A DAD?

Male emperor penguins care for their chicks during the bitter Antarctic winter. As soon as the female lays the egg, she's off to feed—leaving Dad in charge for two months! He protects the egg and keeps it warm by balancing it on his feet and covering it with a flap of warm skin called a brood pouch. By the time Mom returns, the chick has hatched and Dad has lost around 40 percent of his body weight.

Chick nursery:

Adult penguins taking care of their chicks often huddle together in large colonies to keep warm. Each chick stands on the feet of either its dad or its mom—when she returns—until it is strong enough to cope with the cold Antarctic ice.

QUESTIONS ABOUT
POLAR BEARS

Get answers to your questions about the world's biggest hunter on land.

Polar bears are white, aren't they?

Not really! A polar bear's skin is black, while its outer layer of fur is see-through. Made up of hollow hairs that measure 2–6 in. (5–15 cm) long, a polar bear's fur reflects the light, making it look white.

How do polar bears get around?

Polar bears can sprint at 25 mph (40 km/h), but only for short distances. The soles of a bear's feet have small bumps and troughs that act like suction cups, keeping them from slipping on the ice. Polar bears are surprisingly good swimmers; they can reach speeds of 6 mph (10 km/h), mostly using their front legs to paddle.

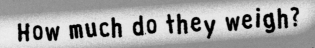

How much do they weigh?

An adult male polar bear can weigh over 1,320 lb. (600 kg)—that's more than six adult humans! When they are born, it is a different story. A cub is 12–14 in. (30–35 cm) long and weighs around 18 oz. (500 g)—that's about the size of a guinea pig!

How do polar bears deal with the cold?

Two layers of fur covering a thick layer of body fat, called **blubber**, help **insulate** polar bears from the biting cold weather. A short tail, ears, and snout also help by giving off less heat. Sometimes, when winds are especially fierce, polar bears will dig pits in snow banks and curl up into a tight ball inside.

PECULIAR
POLAR CREATURES

Presenting the top 10 seriously strange things living in the waters of the polar regions!

1 Lion's mane jellyfish

This GIANT jellyfish has a dome that can grow to 6.5 ft. (2 m) wide with up to 1,200 tentacles, which it uses to sting and capture prey.

The tentacles can grow to 108 ft. (33 m) long—that's longer than an NBA basketball court!

Narwhal

This Arctic Ocean porpoise has a giant tooth known as a tusk. This tusk grows through its upper lip to a length of 5–10 ft. (1.5–3.1 m)!

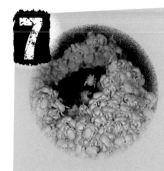

Hoff crab

This strange creature, found in Antarctica's waters, lets bacteria grow on its chest, then uses comb-like mouthparts to eat them!

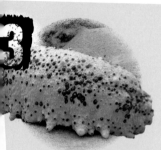

Sea pig

Sea pigs suck up particles from the seabed. Their pink bodies make them look like the animals they are named after—pigs!

Comb jelly

This Arctic jellyfish has rows of moving hairs that push it through the water. The hairs reflect light—making the jelly sparkle!

Basket star

These strange-looking sea creatures grow tangled masses of arms, all covered in tiny, sharp hooks that help them catch prey.

Ice worms

Spending all their lives in glaciers, these worms are so used to the cold that if you warm them up to just 41°F (5°C), they turn to liquid!

Hooded seal

Males of this deep-diving Arctic seal have a balloon-like sac that can be blown up out of one of their nostrils to make sounds that impress the females.

Arctic lamprey

These funny fish have a sucking mouth with teeth, which they use to latch on to bigger fish and suck out tasty blood to feed on!

Southern Ocean giant sea spider

Sea spiders in Antarctica are huge. They have eight long, spindly legs, which span up to 13.8 in. (35 cm).

Which peculiar creature is your number one?

SPERM WHALES have been watched sleeping in the ocean "standing up."

WHALE
OF A TIME!

Enjoy these facts about the biggest creatures found in the polar oceans!

- The biggest creature on Earth is the **BLUE WHALE**.

- **KILLER WHALES** (orcas) are really a type of dolphin.

- **BLUE WHALES** feed on tiny, shrimplike creatures called krill.

- **GRAY WHALES** travel 5,000–7,000 mi. (8,000–11,000 km) across the **equator** to the Arctic in the summer, then back to the Antarctic when winter looms.

- The biggest brain in the animal kingdom belongs to the **SPERM WHALE**.

A **BLUE WHALE'S** tongue weighs more than 2 tons and is big enough for an entire soccer team to stand on.

- **HUMPBACK WHALES** work as a team to blow bubbles that form a kind of net around a shoal of tasty fish or krill.

POLAR PEOPLE

ARCTIC PEOPLES

Just over four million people live within the Arctic Circle. Many of them have moved to the Arctic to work in the fishing, oil and gas, or tourism industries. Others are descendants of traditional Arctic peoples, who have lived in the region for centuries.

Nenets

Greenland

GREENLAND is home to 57,000 people. Its small towns and villages are famous for their brightly colored houses. People often travel by boat or by dogsled because there aren't many roads.

FROZEN FACT

Found mostly in Alaska, northern Canada, and Greenland, the **INUIT** hunt seals, whales, and fish, which they eat cooked or raw. They used to live in tents made of animal skins in the summer while in the winter, some built igloos out of snow blocks.

FROZEN FACT

Inuit

Sami

SAMI people live in parts of Finland, Norway, Sweden, and Russia. Their traditional *gákti* dress used to be made from reindeer skin, but today most clothes are made of cotton or wool.

FROZEN FACT

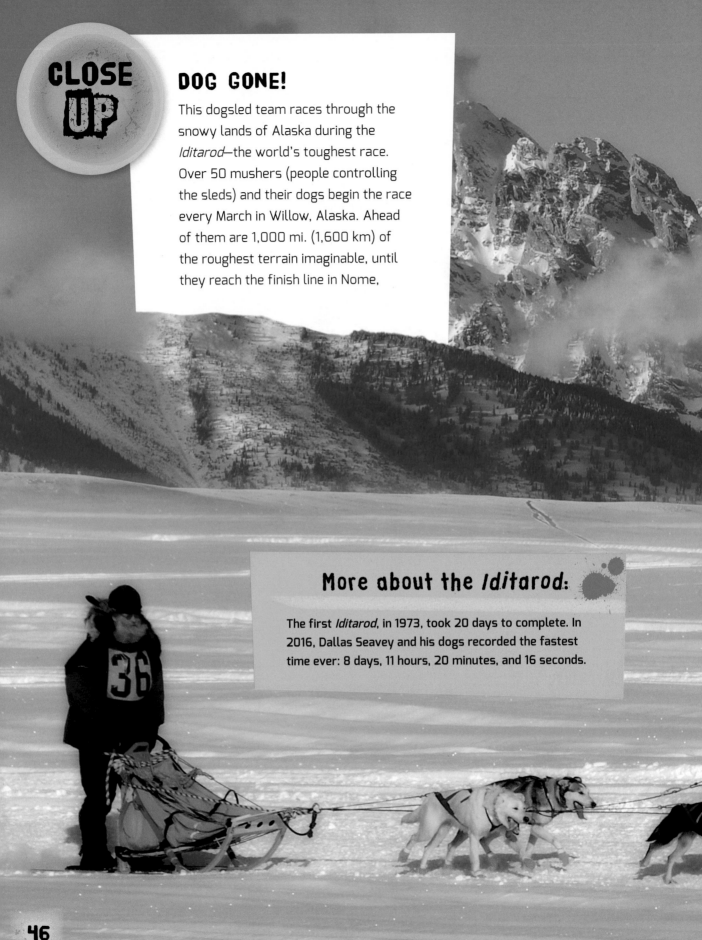

DOG GONE!

This dogsled team races through the snowy lands of Alaska during the *Iditarod*—the world's toughest race. Over 50 mushers (people controlling the sleds) and their dogs begin the race every March in Willow, Alaska. Ahead of them are 1,000 mi. (1,600 km) of the roughest terrain imaginable, until they reach the finish line in Nome,

More about the *Iditarod*:

The first *Iditarod*, in 1973, took 20 days to complete. In 2016, Dallas Seavey and his dogs recorded the fastest time ever: 8 days, 11 hours, 20 minutes, and 16 seconds.

Socks keep their paws warm!

TOP 10

POLAR EXPLORERS

Check out these champion explorers of the poles.

1 Roald Amundsen

Discoverer of a sea passage between Greenland and Canada (1903–1906), this brave Norwegian became the first person to reach the South Pole (1911). He was also first to fly over the North Pole (1926).

Fridtjof Hansen

The first person to ski across Greenland (1888), this explorer was also first to sail across the whole Arctic Ocean (1893).

Norman D. Vaughan

Vaughan explored the Antarctic in 1930 with Richard Byrd and, 64 years later, returned to climb Mount Vaughan—a mountain named after him!

Ranulph Fiennes

This explorer has made more than 30 **expeditions** to the polar regions. In 1993, he made the first unsupported walk across Antarctica.

Edgeworth David

Living off seals and penguins in Antarctica, David (centre) led the first expedition to climb the continent's only active volcano, Mount Erebus.

Ann Bancroft

Bancroft was the first woman to reach the North Pole on foot and sled (1986) and the first to ski across Antarctica (2001).

James Clark Ross

This sailor was the first to sail around almost all of the coast of Antarctica (1839–1843), establishing that it is a continent.

Ernest Shackleton

Shackleton made four expeditions to Antarctica (1901–1922). He explored the Transantarctic Mountains and carried out a heroic rescue in 1915–1916.

David Hempleman-Adams

This explorer gained the first "grand slam": reaching both poles and climbing the highest mountain on every continent!

Vivian Fuchs

Fuchs led the first expedition to cross the continent of Antarctica, in 1958. The expedition used tractors to cover 2,158 mi. (3,473 km) in 99 days.

Which brave explorer is your number one?

Norwegian team

RACE TO THE SOUTH POLE

THE NORWEGIAN EXPEDITION

TEAM FACTS

Leader: Roald Engelbregt Gravning Amundsen (1872–1928)
Ship: *Fram*
Sailed From: Kristiania (now called Oslo), Norway
Arrived in Antarctica: January 1911
Base: Framheim, Bay of Whales

Amundsen set out with four other men and 52 dogs in October 1911. At first they managed to cover 25 mi. (40 km) a day, but as the journey grew more difficult, they slowed down. The five had to make their way across a glacier criss-crossed with dozens of cracks and gaps, but on December 14, 1911, they planted a Norwegian flag at the South Pole. They returned safely to their base, Framheim, after 99 days and nearly 1,860 mi. (3,000 km) of adventuring.

Amundsen made his base 60 mi. (96 km) closer to the South Pole than the British team, led by Scott. Amundsen's men were all good skiers, and they were equipped with warm fur clothing, similar to that used by Inuit people in the Arctic. Amundsen's team had sleds like those of his rival, Scott, but modified them so they weighed only a quarter of the weight. This meant that the Arctic husky dogs needed to make less effort to pull them.

amazing Antarctica

In June 1910, two ships left Europe for the Antarctic. Both carried expeditions led by men intent on being the first to reach the South Pole. The race to be first was on!

Terra Nova **team**

THE BRITISH EXPEDITION

TEAM FACTS

Leader: Robert Falcon Scott (1868–1912)
Ship: *Terra Nova*
Sailed From: Cardiff, Wales
Arrived in Antarctica: January 1911
Base: Cape Evans, McMurdo Sound

on January 17, 1912, only to discover Amundsen had got there first! They began their 800 mi. (1,300 km)–journey back to safety. It began well, but **blizzards** and temperatures dropping to below –40°F (–40°C) slowed their progress. They suffered from frostbite, exhaustion, and a shortage of supplies. The team perished in March 1912, just 11 mi. (18 km) from a depot full of supplies.

Robert Falcon Scott hoped to reach the South Pole using ponies, dogs, and gasoline-powered motor sleds with tracks like a bulldozer. The motor vehicles and ponies turned out to be unsuited to the harsh Antarctic weather, and the dogsleds, which started out in November, turned back in December.

Scott pressed on, as one of a party of five who pulled their sleds on foot as they climbed a glacier and reached the South Pole

The Observation Hill cross— a memorial for Scott's team

1 In 2014, a rock band played a 30-minute gig on an iceberg floating in the Greenland Sea. Rock on!

TOP 10

POLAR STUNTS

Which are the most EXTREME feats staged at the Poles?

2

Lewis Gordon Pugh swam 0.6 mi. (1 km) in the icy sea close to the North Pole in 2005 wearing just goggles, a swim hat, and his trunks! Yikes!

3

Felicity Aston skied on her own, pulling a sled with a tent and supplies, for 1,084 mi. (1,744 km) across Antarctica. Her epic trek took 59 days!

6 Every November, around 50 extreme athletes trek a 26.2 mi (42.2 km)–long Antarctic Ice Marathon near the foot of the Ellsworth Mountains.

7 A number of daredevils have used kites, which catch the fierce polar winds, to kite-ski across part of either the Arctic ice cap or the Antarctica.

8 Actress and adventurer Manon Ossevoort drove her Massey Ferguson tractor 1,550 mi. (2,500 km) to the South Pole In 2014!

4 in 2013, Ramon Navarro became the first person to surf in the Antarctic region off the coast of the South Shetland Islands. Brrr!

9 In 2007, TV car show hosts Jeremy Clarkson and James May drove to the North Pole in two modified Toyota pickup trucks.

5 Maria Leijerstam reached the South Pole on a special bicycle! She pedaled 396 mi. (638 km) on a bike equipped with skis and balloon tires that were 4.5 in. (11.3 cm) wide.

10 David Beckham flew to Antarctica in 2015 and played a soccer match on Union Glacier with staff at the base there. The game ended 3–3.

BREAKING THE ICE

The Russian icebreaker NS *Yamal* crunches through heavy ice in the Arctic Ocean. Icebreakers are strong and sturdy ships that break up ice to let other ships through or to reach and rescue vessels stuck in the ice. Built in 1992, *Yamal* is as long as one and a half soccer fields and is powered by two nuclear reactors. This means it can sail for five years before it needs to refuel.

More about NS *Yamal*:

The front of the ship, called the prow, is made of extrathick steel (19 in. / 48 cm thick) to withstand impact with the ice. *Yamal*'s sister ship, *Arktika*, was the first ship to muscle through the ice to reach the geographic North Pole in 1977.

Be amazed at
these incredible
survival stories!

SURVIVAL

CAUGHT IN A CREVASSE

FROZEN FACT

Where: Inland from Commonwealth Bay, Antarctica

When: 1912–1913

Expedition leader: Douglas Mawson

Mawson

Australian Douglas Mawson was left alone more than 155 mi. (250 km) from safety after both of his team members perished. The first, along with the sled carrying much of their supplies, fell down a deep crack in the ice known as a **crevasse**.

Mawson slowly trekked back through blizzards toward safety, until he fell into a crevasse himself. He was dangling in midair, from a rope attached to his sled, which was wedged in the crevasse above. Below him was certain death . . .

Cold and weak, he pulled himself out of the crevasse's icy jaws and collapsed on the surface. Mawson battled hunger, frostbite, and exhaustion yet managed to reach safety at Cape Denison three weeks later.

"Below was a black chasm. Exhausted, weak, and chilled . . . I hung with the firm conviction that all was over."

Douglas Mawson

STORIES

TRAPPED AND A TREK

Where: Weddell Sea to South Georgia
When: 1914–1916
Expedition leader: Ernest Shackleton

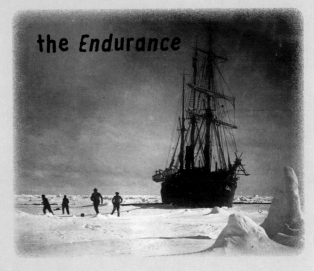

the *Endurance*

Shackleton and his 27-man crew became trapped when their ship, the *Endurance*, got stuck in ice in the Weddell Sea for 10 months. The ship was crushed by the ice and, with no communication or chance of a passing ship, they were in trouble! Shackleton led his crew over the ice, hauling three wooden lifeboats.

Leaving most of the crew on Elephant Island, where they lived off seal meat, Shackleton took five men to sail a lifeboat across more than 745 mi. (1,200 km) of stormy sea to reach South Georgia. The dangerous voyage took 17 days.

Once on South Georgia, Shackleton and two of his crew hiked for 36 hours across glaciers and mountains to find a whaling station on the other side of the island. From there, Shackleton organized rescue attempts, saving the rest of his crew three months later.

> "Our ship crushed and lost and we ourselves drifting on a piece of ice at the mercy of the winds . . ."
>
> Ernest Shackleton

The most southerly base is called **AMUNDSEN-SCOTT** and is right by the South Pole. It holds around 150 people!

ANTARCTIC BASES

Fuel your fascination with Antarctic stations or bases with these great facts.

> All of the **FOOD** eaten at the Amundsen-Scott station has to be flown there by cargo plane.

* There are about **70 PERMANENT BASES** in and around the Antarctic continent.

* The biggest base of all is the United States' **MCMURDO STATION**. It houses up to 1,258 people!

* **OPERATION DEEP FREEZE** sees big ships transport around 11 million lb. (5 million kg) of food and supplies to the McMurdo Station each year.

* **DURING THEIR TIME OFF**, station staff can snap the scenery, go jogging in the snow, ski, or even play ice soccer for exercise.

* The world's most southerly post office is found at the former British base of **PORT LOCKROY**.

THE GREAT POLAR QUIZ

Are you an expert on all things polar? Test your knowledge by completing this quiz! When you've answered all of the questions, turn to page 63 to check your score.

 How many people live in Antarctica permanently
a) 0
b) 500
c) 50,000

 What is the largest ice shelf in Antarctica?
a) Larsen Ice Shelf
b) Nansen Ice Shelf
c) Ross Ice Shelf

Who reached the North Pole by dogsled in 1986?
a) Will Smith
b) Will Steger
c) Willy Wonka

 How many tourists visit Antarctica each year?
a) 5,000
b) 40,000
c) 350,000

 How many meteorites have been found on Antarctica?
a) 18
b) 450
c) More than 20,000

 How big are growler icebergs?
a) the size of a car
b) the size of a house
c) the size of a jumbo jet

 How many icebergs do scientists think are produced in the Arctic Circle each year?
a) 8,000
b) 40,000
c) 2,000,000

 The cerimonial South Pole is marked by what?
a) A blue igloo
b) A red-and-white-striped pole
c) A star-shaped flag

 Which creature turns to liquid if you heat it to 41°F (5°c)?
a) Ice snail
b) Ice snake
c) Ice worm

 How much does a baby polar bear weigh at birth?
a) 0.25 oz. (7 g)
b) 88 lb. (40 kg)
c) 18 oz. (500 g)

 Which creature can eat around 1,600 lemmings a year?
a) Greenland shark
b) Polar bear
c) Snowy owl

 Which flying visitor to the Arctic can dive at speeds of more than 186 mph (300 km/h)?
a) Arctic tern
b) Peregrine falcon
c) Snow goose

 What is the biggest creature on Earth?
a) Beluga whale
b) Blue whale
c) Minke whale

 How long can the tentacles of a lion's mane jellyfish grow to?
a) 13 in. (33 cm)
b) 11 ft. (3.3 m)
c) 108 ft. (33 m)

 Which Arctic mammal's thick coat produces *qiviut* wool?
a) Caribou
b) Musk ox
c) Yak

 How many clams can an adult walrus eat in a day?
a) 100
b) 800
c) 4,000

 How much does a Weddell seal weigh?
a) More than 110 lb. (50 kg)
b) More than 1,100 lb. (500 kg)
c) More than 1,200 lb. (550 kg)

 Which is the biggest and heaviest penguin species?
a) Emperor
b) King
c) Gentoo

 What is the name of the largest scientific base on Antarctica?
a) McMurdo Station
b) Port Lockroy
c) Scott-Amundsen South Pole Station

 In what year did Roald Amundsen reach the South Pole?
a) 1909
b) 1911
c) 1913

 How long can a narwhal's tusk grow to?
a) 5–10 ft. (1.5–3.1 m)
b) 10–15 ft. (3.1–4.6 m)
c) 15–20 ft. (4.6–6.1 m)

GLOSSARY

Arctic Circle
An imaginary line around the northernmost part of Earth. The land and sea above this line is known as the Arctic.

atmosphere
The gases that surround Earth.

blizzard
A heavy snowstorm that comes with high winds.

blubber
A thick layer of fat under the skin that helps keep animals warm.

camouflage
Colors and patterns that blend in with a creature's surroundings, making the creature hard to see.

carnivorous
A meat-eating creature, such as a polar bear, a seal, or a shark.

continent
One of the seven large land masses found on Earth: Africa, Antarctica, Oceania, Asia, Europe, North America, and South America.

crevasse
A deep, usually vertical crack or split in a glacier.

equator
An imaginary line around the middle of the Earth that marks the midpoint between the North Pole and South Pole.

expedition
A journey made by a group of people with a particular aim, such as exploring unmapped lands or performing scientific work.

glacier
A moving river of ice.

hibernation
A deep, sleeplike state that some animals enter through the winter.

iceberg
A large piece of floating ice that has calved, or broken off, from a glacier or ice shelf.

ice shelf
A large amount of ice that is attached to land but extends out into the ocean.

insulate
To surround or cover something to help stop heat loss.

krill
Tiny, shrimplike creatures that live in seas and oceans.

mammal
A warm-blooded animal that feeds its young on milk.

migration
A long journey some animals make each year to a distant place, often to feed and breed, followed by a return trip back.

nomadic
Constantly moving homes instead of living in just one place. People who follow animal migrations are nomadic.

peninsula
A peninsula is an area of land that juts out into the sea and has water on three of its sides.

polar
To do with the regions of the North Pole and South Pole of Earth.

predator
A creature that hunts other creatures for food.

prey
A creature that is hunted for food by other creatures.

tundra
An area where few trees or plants grow because of extremely cold weather and short growing seasons.

QUIZ ANSWERS: 1 = a, 2 = c, 3 = b, 4 = b, 5 = c, 6 = a, 7 = b, 8 = b, 9 = c, 10 = c, 11 = c, 12 = b, 13 = b, 14 = c, 15 = b, 16 = c, 17 = c, 18 = a, 19 = a, 20 = b, 21 = c.

INDEX